Managing Stress

Managing Stress

Kristine C Brewer

Gower

First published in the USA by National Press
Publications Inc.
This edition published by
Gower Publishing Limited
Gower House
Croft Road
Aldershot
Hampshire GU11 3HR
England

British Library Cataloguing in Publication Data
Brewer, Kristine C.
    Managing stress
    1. Stress management
    I. Title
    155.9'042

    ISBN 0 566 07946 1

Typeset in Palatino by Raven Typesetters, Chester
and printed in Great Britain by Biddles Ltd, Guildford.

Contents

Introduction

Stress is unavoidable. Whether it's triggered by an attacking tiger in the prehistoric jungle or by office politics in the corporate jungle, it is a fact of life.

The stress we experience today is more intense and unrelenting than that experienced by our primitive ancestors. When a tiger attacked primitive man, man's body responded with the classic fight or flight reaction. Through dramatic chemical changes, his body physiologically prepared itself for two options: flee or attack. His choices were clear. He was either eaten, in which case ongoing stress wasn't an issue, or he survived and his body

quickly returned to normal. Regardless of the outcome, his body's response to stress was geared to
survival.

In many ways the body's stress response was an
ally and is probably one of the reasons humans
evolved. Today, the stress we experience is less
obvious and more pervasive. For many, stress is not
an ally but the cause of deteriorating health, lack of
productivity or depression. Why? Well, unlike the
tiger encounter, the stress we experience today is not
nearly as tangible. Consequently, our options for
relieving stress aren't as clear cut. We focus on relieving the symptoms rather than locating the cause.
This allows stress to become pervasive in our lives.

Stress is our response to anxiety-producing
events. Stress is a reaction to change. It is a syn-
drome that includes three major responses:

1. mental;
2. emotional;
3. physiological.

Instead of a surge of adrenaline, which gives us the
strength to overcome short-term stress, we experience ongoing stress that continually stimulates
our biochemical stress mechanisms. This flood of
hormones which ensured our survival thousands of
years ago now threatens it through increased heart
attacks, high blood pressure and a variety of other
debilitating ailments.

That's the bad news. The good news is that we

can understand how and why we react to stress. We can then become its master.

Mastering stress is the key to this book. That doesn't mean we need to eliminate it entirely, nor should we wish to. Stress is an integral part of life. It can be a powerful force to produce positive change and enhance productivity.

This book explains how and why we react to stress. Remember, stress management is a highly personal process. This book provides guidance and offers specific ways to create a stress-management programme tailored to meet individual needs and to fit personal styles.

1

Stress fundamentals

After reading this chapter, you will know:

- the definition of stress;

- the common symptoms of stress;

- how to identify stress in the workplace and at home.

Before you begin reading, take a moment to complete the three sentences of your 'wanted poster' (Figure 1.1) to assess your stress level. Ask another person who knows you well to complete the 'caution' section.

1

WANTED

VITAL STATISTICS

Name

Birthplace

Occupation

WANTED for experiencing stress when ...
WANTED for responding to stress by ...
WANTED for using questionable coping tactics such as ...

CAUTION: this person is ...

_____	wild and irresponsible
_____	harmless
_____	a ticking bomb
_____	on the run
_____	on probation
_____	hard to pin down
_____	clever
_____	intense
_____	armed with great personal strength
_____	wanted in several states of consciousness
_____	scattered in many directions
_____	AWOL from work for a day
_____	known to be very responsible
_____	in hot pursuit of the meaning of life
_____	not guilty by reason of insanity
_____	about to snap someone's head off
_____	hazardous to their health
_____	DWI (driven with imagination)
_____	other _____
_____	other _____

Figure 1.1   'Wanted for stress' poster

Stress: what it is

What do we think of when we hear the word 'stress'? One thing is certain – there are as many different ideas about stress as there are people who experience change in their lives. Stress, quite simply, is the way we react, physically and emotionally, to change. Like change, stress can be either positive or negative. Stress may be the sense of concentration we feel when faced with a new and challenging situation; it may be the vague sense of anxiety we feel after 'one of those days'. In any case, we *can* learn to manage stress so that we can be in control.

Positive stress

In its positive aspect, stress helps us to concentrate, focus and perform, and can often help us to reach peak efficiency. Many people, in fact, do their best work when under pressure. Then, when the challenge has been met, they take the time to relax and enjoy their achievements. This relaxation response allows them to build up the physical and emotional reserves to meet the next challenge. It is one of the key elements of positive stress.

Negative stress

Stress becomes negative when we stay geared up and won't – or can't – relax after meeting the challenge. In today's world, where many situations can 'push our buttons', it's no wonder some people think of stress as a way of life. Unfortunately, when stress becomes a constant, ongoing cycle, health and wellbeing can suffer. Negative stress has been linked with many physical ailments, from tension headaches to heart attacks. The good news: stress needn't be hazardous to our health. We can learn to manage the stress in our lives and be happy that we did!

Three types of stress

Stress can take three forms:

1. physical stress;

2. mental stress;

3. emotional stress.

Physical stress

Physical stress – the closest thing to the attack by a tiger – is an immediate threat to our physical being: traffic accidents, a physical injury, being attacked in the street, etc.

Physical stress triggers our body's fight or flight biochemical mechanism. Released adrenaline tenses our muscles, dilates our pupils and increases our heart rates. Once the stressful situation is overcome, our body returns to normal, and we stop producing adrenaline.

Mental stress

Mental stress is much more complicated, because:

- it is harder to identify;

- it usually involves complex issues which are further compounded by behaviours and emotions that are difficult to view objectively;

- it often involves other people and their emotions, values and behaviours.

Emotional stress

Emotional stress is so difficult to cope with because it can unsettle us in one or more of four basic areas, specifically when:

1. something threatens our beliefs, values, security, or wellbeing;

2. we try to adjust to change;

3. we lose control and feel vulnerable and helpless;

4. our expectations are not realized.

Causes of mental stress

People, situations or events that cause us mental stress do so for one of four reasons:

1. *We feel threatened.* This can threaten our values, our personal or financial security, our wellbeing or other key aspects of our lives. These are pressures from which we may feel there is no escape.

2. *We experience change.* Regardless of whether the change is positive or negative, major changes in our lives are stressful.

3. *We lose our sense of control.* A sense of helplessness and vulnerability is extremely stressful to most people. A good example is the loss of a job or a serious illness.

4. *Our expectations aren't realized.* Regardless of whether our expectations (about jobs, other people, situations or whatever) are realistic, when they aren't met we can experience a great deal of mental stress. When people or situations conflict with our values, however indirectly or subtly, we experience stress.

Responses to stress

Whether the cause of stress is mental or physical, we can respond in three basic ways:

1. *Resist.* We can fight the tiger, our colleagues, our spouses. In this case, we view stress as an assault by an external source and we respond defensively.

2. *Avoid.* We can bury our heads in the sand and hope whatever is making us feel bad will give up and go away. A common avoidance technique is reliance on alcohol or drugs.

3.   *Confront/adapt.* We can work to identify the real cause of our stress and eliminate it. If this is not possible, then we work out how to adapt so it won't destroy our lives.

The good, bad and ugly forms of stress

Since challenge to some is stress to others, the key is our ability to turn stressful situations into positive opportunities.

Positive stress

So-called 'good stress' doesn't refer to a particular situation or event but to how an individual reacts to it. (Getting a new job and being assigned a particularly challenging project are examples of good stress.) If we experience good stress, we tend to feel:

● sharply focused;

● energized;

● motivated;

● aware of options;

● challenged.

Positive stress can help us concentrate and focus. It can also help us to survive. Our physical stress response helps us to meet challenging (or threatening) situations. It is an automatic and essential fact of life.

Our stress (arousal) response is automatic when faced with a challenging situation:

- muscles tense;
- heart pounds;
- blood pressure rises;
- hands become cold and clammy;
- stomach tenses.

When stress is positive, our body automatically relaxes after we've handled the situation that caused the stress response:

- muscles relax;
- heart beats normally;
- blood pressure lowers;
- hands become warm and dry;
- stomach relaxes.

Bad stress

Bad stress is often caused by the incident or individual who produces the last straw in an already difficult day. (A flat tyre that makes you late for an important meeting is a good example.) With bad stress we tend to feel:

- tense;
- anxious;
- angry or depressed;
- like withdrawing or lashing out;

● frustrated.

Negative stress

This is a chronic, pervasive and often subtle form of bad stress. It occurs when we feel taken advantage of for an extended period of time, uncertain about our future or burdened by financial difficulties. This negative stress causes:

● lack of energy;

● chronic depression;

● health problems;

● low self-esteem.

Our physical (alarm-stage) reaction to stress is always the same, but with negative stress our body stays geared up and doesn't relax. When stress becomes chronic and ongoing, our physical and emotional health suffers.

Our automatic physical reaction to a stressful situation is the same whether we experience positive or negative stress. Positive and negative stress share the same response mechanism, but in negative stress our response stays stuck in the on position – we can't quite turn it off.

Look at Table 1.1 and indicate the degree to which each item gives you stress. What does your profile look like? What are the two most important items to improve on? Which ones are under control?

With negative stress, there is no true relaxation

Table 1.1   Stress profile

Cause of stress	Low stress		Moderate stress		High Stress
1. Lack of time to do things you want or need to do	1	2	3	4	5
2. The balance of work and family life	1	2	3	4	5
3. Lack of recreation or socializing	1	2	3	4	5
4. Frustration with dreams or goals	1	2	3	4	5
5. Lack of support	1	2	3	4	5
6. No direction or purpose	1	2	3	4	5
7. Feeling of being trapped in a situation	1	2	3	4	5
8. Monotony	1	2	3	4	5
9. Conflicting schedules	1	2	3	4	5

between one stress crisis and the next. When our bodies remain geared up, physical and emotional strain can result. Fortunately, we can stop the cycle of negative stress by becoming aware of our stress (and how we react to it), by practising relaxation techniques and by developing a positive attitude and life-style.

The difference in how we react to stress depends largely on how we perceive ourselves and our situation.

Common stress symptoms

No matter how hard we try, we can't keep it locked inside or ignore it. Doctors estimate that 75 per cent of all medical complaints are stress related. The most common complaints include:

- insomnia/sleep disorders;
- sexual dysfunction;
- indigestion/vomiting;
- ulcers/diarrhoea;
- headaches;
- muscle aches;
- high blood pressure/heart attacks/strokes;
- chronic illnesses (flu, colds, etc.);
- hives.

At least 50 per cent of the population suffers from at least one of these stress symptoms on a regular basis.

Is stress affecting your health?

Answer 'yes', 'no' or 'sometimes' to the following questions.

- Do you wake frequently during the night?
- Is it hard to get to sleep?
- Do you feel like crying or hiding from the world?
- Do you suffer from headaches?
- Do you have high blood pressure?
- Do you experience indigestion after eating?
- Are you tired?

What trend(s) do you see?

Too many people rely on medication to treat symptoms of stress. While medicines may relieve the immediate discomfort, they do nothing to eliminate the stress source. In the meantime, the body's immune system is impaired by the continual release of stress hormones.

The release of adrenaline in response to short-term stress (avoiding the car that almost hit you) doesn't generally harm the immune system. The chemical cortisol is produced when we experience ongoing stress. Overwork and anxiety may result in hormonal imbalance, which can cause exhaustion or sluggishness. This hormone reduces the ability of our immune system to fight disease.

Symptoms of ongoing stress include:

- isolation from family and friends;
- drug/alcohol abuse;
- increase in smoking;
- depression/anxiety;
- irritability/rapid mood swings;
- compulsive eating/dieting;
- child/spouse abuse.

Where stress hits the hardest

There are three key areas of our lives where stress can hit the hardest:

1. personal/home;
2. work/career;
3. financial.

If we experience stress in two or more areas simultaneously, then it is easy to become overwhelmed. An example might be a job loss which results in little or no income at a time when you have major expenses.

Stress is contagious. If we experience continuous,

intense stress in one area – marital problems, having a family member who is terminally ill or severe, unresolved conflicts at work – then we can become so overwhelmed by tension and anxiety that stress can infect all other areas of our lives.

This is why stress management skills are so important. If we experience severe stress in our personal lives, the last thing we need is to have that stress infect our work lives and jeopardize our careers.

In subsequent chapters we'll look at these three key areas, typical forms of stress and options for effective management.

Stress in the workplace

Recent statistics show that 75 per cent of workers indicate they feel stress on the job.

Table 1.2 shows some of the most common stress issues and complaints.

Problems arise when stress in the workplace becomes the rule rather than the exception.

To determine if you have crossed over the line from productive, occasional stress to chronic, debilitating stress, answer the following questions.

Your attitude to work

1. Do you dread going to work?

2. Do you find yourself taking more days off sick, arriving late and leaving early?

3. Do you feel tired at work?

Table 1.2 Most common stress issues and complaints

Basic issue	Symptom or complaint
Lack of control	Undefined job responsibilities, responsible for intermediate step in process but not the final product, not having adequate resources to do job
Lack of recognition or feedback	No method for performance evaluation, no reward or incentive programme, employees feel taken for granted
Uncertainty about future	Concerns about job security, conflicting messages from top management, too many supervisors, unexplained changes in workplace (lay-offs, mergers, drop in sales, etc.)
Boredom	Skills are underutilized, lack of priorities, sloppy work

4. Do you suffer from forgetfulness about work-related tasks or commitments?

5. Do you procrastinate?

6. Do you feel, or does your boss comment, that your performance is below normal?

Evaluate your answers

1. Your attitude towards work as you begin the day is a key indicator of your work environment. If you dread going to work or develop knots in your stomach as you get ready to leave, you definitely need to identify and change whatever causes stress in your work environment.

2. People who take days off sick when they are not ill do so to avoid something at work that bothers them. The same holds true when you arrive late, take long lunches or count the minutes until 5 p.m.

3. How do you know if you are genuinely tired or experiencing stress-related fatigue? The fatigue is stress related if your energy level rebounds when you remove yourself from the stressful environment or situation.

4–6. These questions relate to your ability to get things done at work. A change in your productivity and work habits can be a red flag alerting you to stress. The questions you have to answer are 'Why?' and 'How do I solve the problem?'.

Continue by assessing stress and your work culture.

Your work environment

1. Does the corporate culture where you work encourage a pressure-cooker environment?

2. Are your job responsibilities, and to whom you report, clearly defined?

3. Do you get regular feedback which helps you do your job better?

4. Do you have the support systems (either people or equipment) to carry out your job efficiently and successfully?

5. Do you feel uncertain about your job or the stability of the company?

Evaluate your answers

1. Some companies equate maximum productivity with pressure. Some managers also feel this is a good way to weed out all but the most productive, highly motivated employees. These organizations often create stress both in the work environment and at home. The message they send employees is that work always comes before personal commitments.

   You have the following option:

● Decide if the experience, compensation or prestige is worth the cost in terms of your health and possible damage to your personal life.

2. One of the most widespread causes of stress in the workplace is poorly defined job responsibilities. The key stressor here is lack of control. Close on the heels of this problem is having too many supervisors or not knowing to whom you report. Both situations cause you to receive conflicting instructions or priorities.
   You have the following option:

● Get some answers: a written job description and clarification about to whom you report.

3. Without feedback on your performance, you can easily become frustrated. The issue here is recognition. Feedback can be informal (a spontaneous conversation with your boss) or formal (a performance review).
   These are your options.

● Establish short-term, measurable goals (increase in sales, number of items produced, etc.) with supervisors.

● Establish times to review progress and get feedback.

4. Knowing you can do a job well and being prevented from doing so because of lack of support creates tremendous stress. The key issue here is lack of control.

    You have these options.

    ● Identify what resources you lack to do your job efficiently and successfully.

    ● Justify the need for these resources in terms of benefits to the company (increased sales, better customer service, faster order fulfilment, etc.).

5. Worrying about job security produces unrelenting stress. If you are worried about the future of your job or company, you can regain a sense of control by building a 'lifeboat'.

    A lifeboat represents work alternatives in the event of your losing your job. Identifying these options in advance of a crisis puts you in control.

    ● Work out the minimum income needed to meet monthly obligations.

    ● List all the ways you can earn money.

    ● List what you would like to do for a living.

    ● Look for ways these lists overlap.

    ● Develop realistic short-term alternatives and long-term goals to strive for.

Stress at home

Three basic areas where people typically experience stress in their personal lives are:

1. interpersonal relationships with family members;

2. balancing career and family obligations;

3. coping with financial problems.

The stress of relating to others

Close relationships (with spouse, parents, children, room-mates, etc.) inevitably produce stress. As we discussed earlier, much of this stress is caused by unrealistic expectations.

Another important factor is the roles people assume or allow to be placed on them by others. Nowhere is this more common (nor does it produce more stress in many households) than among married couples.

Stress, burnout or pressure?

Burnout and pressure, in the corporate world, can be badges of honour. Many people talk about how much pressure they are under. The implication is that these individuals are overworked because they are important and have been entrusted with a signif-icant amount of responsibility. (Some corporate cultures even create an atmosphere of continual

pressure in an attempt to make their employees productive.)

Admitting to stress, on the other hand, is perceived by many as a display of weakness. While this
notion is changing, various surveys indicate that
women feel more comfortable using the term 'stress'
to describe feelings of anxiety, tension, extended
depression or being overwhelmed. Men are more
comfortable describing these symptoms as pressure
or burnout. Stress is commonly perceived as weakness or vulnerability, the inability to handle pressure; burnout is perceived as mental or physical
exhaustion from working too hard; and pressure is
perceived as being overwhelmed by multiple or conflicting responsibilities.

Whatever we call it, prolonged stress/burnout/
pressure, it is not healthy and should not be touted
as an essential element of a successful career.

Coping mechanisms: are they solving the problem or just hiding it?

Generally we cope by working through four phases:

1. *Hope it will go away.* This is the 'burying
   your head in the sand' approach to coping.
   At this stage the stress isn't causing enough
   pain to make it worth the effort to do something about it.

2. *Seek fast relief.* This is the stage where most
   people turn to medication, alcohol, drugs or

other means to numb themselves against the unpleasant physical or mental discomforts of stress.

3. *Take it out on others.* If we are under stress, our spouse or children can be particularly annoying. Taking out our stress on others can range from lashing out with an angry comment to physical abuse.

4. *Seek help.* If we are lucky, we get to this phase. Help can include the use of stress management techniques, discussing feelings with a spouse or close friend who can help us gain perspective or seeking professional counselling.

Most people don't plan stress-coping skills ahead of time. The keys to stress management (effective coping) are:

● identify the stress source;

● have a stress management strategy in place that offers a step-by-step method to relieve the symptoms and eliminate the cause;

● have outside support (family, friends, counsellors, etc.) available.

How are you using coping mechanisms?

Identify a current cause of stress and identify which coping stage you are currently in and what one thing will help you get to Phase 4 to get the stress under control.

Summary

- We experience three basic types of stress: physical, mental and emotional. Physical stress tends to be a short-term threat, and usually our response choices are clear cut. Mental stress is harder to identify and manage. It often spills over into (or is manifested by) emotional stress. We encounter mental and emotional stress most often.

- Mental and emotional stress are difficult to cope with because they can unsettle us in one or more of four basic areas; when:

  1. something threatens our beliefs, values, security or well-being;

  2. we try to adjust to change;

  3. we lose control and feel vulnerable and helpless;

  4. our expectations are not realized.

- There are three basic ways we can respond to stress:

  1. resist;

  2. avoid;

  3. confront/adapt.

- We all internalize stress, but we can't avoid or ignore its negative effects.

● The most common symptoms of stress are physical and behavioural problems. Physical problems usually take the form of illnesses or various aches and pains. Behavioural problems range from isolating oneself to physical abuse.

● Stress hits us the hardest in three key areas: our personal lives (home, family, friends), work and financial matters.

● Failure to deal with ongoing stress in one area increases the risk of it affecting other areas of our lives.

● Is there a difference between stress, burnout and pressure? Stress can be associated with weakness and an inability to cope, while burnout and pressure can be seen as by-products of professional achievement.

● We cope with stress in four phases:

   1. hope it will go away;

   2. seek fast, temporary relief;

   3. take it out on others;

   4. seek help.

2

Managing stress: priorities and perspective

After reading this chapter, you will know:

- how priorities help us avoid stress;
- how to identify work and personal priorities;
- how to accept change to minimize stress.

Too often stress becomes a negative cycle. Unresolved, chronic stress quickly spreads from one area of our lives to others and back and forth between the people with whom we interact.

Why do some people seem to experience more

stress than others or seem to experience stress in situations that leave other people unaffected? It has to do largely with how individuals manage three fundamental elements of their lives:

1. priorities;
2. expectations;
3. coping with change.

Answer yes or no to the following questions.

1. Are you constantly doing more than one thing at a time?

2. When travelling, do you feel the travel time is wasted?

3. Do you get angry when things don't run smoothly?

4. Do you feel you never manage to finish one thing before moving on to the next?

5. Are you constantly being told you work too hard?

6. Do you work more than ten hours on a work day?

7. Are you too busy to develop a creative outlet, such as gardening or needlework?

8. Do you take less than half an hour for meals or skip them?

9. Are you too busy to go outside each day for at least half an hour?

10. Do you get less than seven hours of sleep at night?

If you answered yes to most of the questions, begin to evaluate time management principles. Time management and not setting priorities could be a cause of stress for you.

How priorities help us to avoid stress

Priorities help us to avoid stress in three ways; by:

1. giving us a way to evaluate a potentially stressful situation;

2. giving us the means to make difficult decisions in a stressful situation;

3. providing us with a valuable sense of perspective when stress threatens to overwhelm us.

Priorities at home and at work transcend the daily crises and hassles and endure for the long haul. Without priorities, we are not firmly grounded, and our day-to-day stability is threatened. That's why we are easily overwhelmed by stressful events that erode our sense of confidence and certainty. Begin immediately to use time management practices.

Assess your priorities

Consider the following questions.

1. What are your long-term career goals? (Own your own business? Reaching a particular management level?)

2. What do you want/need to accomplish at work in the next six months to further your career goals?

3. What conflicts, if any, exist between your goals and your work routine?

4. What are your personal goals? (To spend time with your family? To further your education? To be involved in volunteer work?)

5. What prevents you from pursuing these goals as part of your daily routine?

6. Do you find time to pursue your personal interests on a regular basis?

7. Do you find yourself reacting to others' needs (or demands) and continually putting them before your own?

8. How many roles do you play during the day? (husband/wife, executive/secretary, father/mother, adult/child)

9. What priority conflicts exist between different roles?

10. Do you feel you manage your time well? Why?

Interpretation

Questions 1–3 examine work priorities. These priorities should not be defined exclusively by others (colleagues, managers, etc.).

Our priorities should be defined in terms of work and career goals. Deadlines relate to particular tasks, and job responsibilities relate to the obligations we have to our employers.

Defining priorities will help us:

- avoid a considerable amount of long-term job stress;

- tolerate short-term job stress because our sights will be set on the future;

- know when to change jobs as part of a strategy, not as a reaction to stress.

We can organize our career priorities by:

- identifying what we enjoy, what we do best and what we have experienced;

- setting long-range goals for career achievement;

- setting financial/compensation goals;

- evaluating what role our current position plays in meeting our goals and interests.

Questions 4–9 examine personal priorities and relationships with key people in our lives. A lack of priorities in this area results in:

- frustration because we find ourselves trying to be all things to all people;

- confusion, tension and anxiety because of conflict that exists among the many roles we try to fulfil;

- anger because we fail to meet our own needs.

Keep personal priorities simple. They are most easily organized in terms of:

- the quality of relationships we want with others;

- the obligation we have to meet our own needs (education, hobbies, etc.);

- the commitment we want to make outside work and family (volunteer work, associations, etc.)

Establishing personal priorities will relieve stress by:

- giving us an objective means for evaluating demands made on our time and a basis for saying no to demands that conflict with our priorities;

- simplifying the roles we play (husband/wife, father/mother, career person, caretaker, etc.);

- giving us the means objectively to balance important decisions between career and family life.

Question 10 relates to time management. Good time management will:

- give us the maximum opportunity to exercise all our work and personal priorities;

- give us control over our decisions;

- provide a positive structure to operate within each day.

The keys to practising good time management are to:

- find one time management system that is convenient to use – a good time management system allows us not only to keep track of appointments but also to organize important aspects of our life (work projects, deadlines, telephone calls, long-range planning, etc.);

- pick a system that is portable so we can use it at home and at work;

- use the system daily, asking ourselves constantly, 'Is this the best use of my time right now?'.

Stay flexible

We may work hard to establish priorities only to find that realizing those priorities in daily life is difficult. This happens for two reasons.

First, sometimes the priorities people establish are not really priorities but long-term goals. Priorities are flexible enough to withstand the rigours of daily life. Goals are ideal situations we strive for.

Second, we create more stress when we are not flexible. Be prepared to adapt to minor setbacks.

Our expectations and stress

When we decide people are going to behave in a particular way and we make decisions based on this assumption, we can experience tremendous disappointment if their behaviour fails to live up to our expectations.

We can avoid stress in dealing with others by establishing realistic and mutually compatible expectations. Do this through clear communication in taking the following steps:

1. identify expectations and how others will meet them;

2. determine if the other person is capable of meeting our expectations;

3. discuss our expectations with the other person and determine if she is interested in meeting them;

4. get the other person to summarize the agreement (to avoid misunderstanding on both parts);

5. agree to a deadline for fulfiling the commitment;

6. evaluate, if necessary, to determine whether the commitment was fulfilled.

The burden of perfection

We can also create unrealistic expectations that relate to self-image. Stress is virtually guaranteed when we try to be the:

- perfect employee;
- perfect husband/wife;
- perfect host/hostess;
- perfect parent.

Perfectionism is a no-win situation. Establishing priorities with realistic expectations helps combat perfectionism. To assess your own degree of perfectionism, identify a specific task or situation and then consider the following questions:

1. What effort is required so my commitments to others are satisfied?

2. Are my expectations about the amount of time and quality required consistent with performance standards or the effort others typically need to do a good job?

3. Will spending additional time and energy on this project make a significant difference to the outcome?

4. Do I worry excessively about how others judge my performance?

5. Does this prevent me from finishing tasks on time?

We create unnecessary stress when we try to do everything perfectly. First, it's impossible, so we set ourselves up for failure. Second, no one else expects it.

We will find tasks much less stressful if we:

● realize we will make mistakes, and give ourselves enough time to correct them before the project deadline;

● understand that our knowledge and skills increase more rapidly if we view mistakes as a learning experience;

● realize that having quality work completed on time is better than striving for perfection and completing the project late.

Trying to be something we're not

Another common self-expectation that causes considerable stress is trying to live up to a role or image that isn't compatible with our skills, personality or values.

Often such a role or image is a result of what we feel we 'should' be.

If we can honestly identify personal and career priorities, an unrealistic role becomes obvious. These same priorities help to define an image or role that better fits our personality and value system.

Stress and change

Change is inevitable. If we resist it, we create stress more harmful to us than the change itself.

When you encounter change, remember the three basic ways we can respond to stress.

Resist

We can resist and fight to maintain the status quo. This reaction requires a tremendous amount of time and energy and produces ongoing stress.

Avoid

Avoiding change is a form of passive resistance. It happens when we experience change but fail to acknowledge it. A good example is people who fail to admit that a family member has a serious or terminal illness. When we resist change, we fight back directly. When we avoid change, we don't even acknowledge that we are fighting, yet we experience continual stress because we are engaged in conflict.

Confront/adapt

To confront and then adapt to change is the healthy response which minimizes stress. Change then becomes an opportunity for us, not a danger.

Summary

- How we manage three fundamental elements of our lives dramatically affects the way we react to stressful situations:

  1. priorities;

  2. expectations;

  3. coping with change.

- Clearly defining personal and professional priorities reduces stress. Priorities give us:

  1. a way to evaluate stressful situations;

  2. a basis for making difficult decisions;

  3. a sense of perspective.

- Priorities are based on what is fundamentally important in our lives at home and at work.

- Defining personal and professional priorities helps reduce stress by:

  1. giving us long-term direction and purpose;

2. allowing us to tolerate short-term stress by focusing on the future;

3. helping us understand we can't be all things to all people;

4. defining a more realistic set of roles for ourselves;

5. allowing us to meet more of our own needs.

● We need to organize our personal priorities in terms of:

1. the quality of relationships we want (friends, family, etc.);

2. obligations to meet our own needs;

3. commitments outside the work and family.

● Essential to stress management is good time management. Practicing good time management allows us to:

1. have maximum options in terms of work and home priorities;

2. have a sense of control;

3. reinforce priorities;

4. have a positive structure to function in each day.

- A good time management system:

    1. is easy and convenient to use;

    2. is portable, so it can be used at home and in the office;

    3. allows us to reschedule our time, organize, meet deadlines and plan.

- Be flexible. Don't establish priorities and then try to rigidly adhere to them. Be prepared to accept minor setbacks.

- Often we have unrealistic expectations of others – we expect them to behave based on our wants.

- Establish realistic expectations of others by:

    1. identifying our own needs;

    2. determining if the other person can meet them;

    3. discussing our needs to see if the other person wants to meet them;

    4. summarizing our mutual expectations;

    5. identifying a deadline for fulfilment of the obligation;

    6. evaluating the outcome, if appropriate.

- Perfectionism is another major cause of stress. We can avoid this by:

1. realizing that mistakes are normal and allowing time to correct them;

2. understanding that making mistakes can increase our knowledge and skills;

3. realizing that a quality product which meets a deadline is more important than a perfect product which is late or never finished.

● Trying to be something we are not is a self-expectation that causes considerable stress.

● Learn to confront and adapt to major and minor changes. We must learn to accept change so we can minimize a great deal of stress.

3

The importance of communication in stress management

After reading this chapter, you will know:

- three ways to communicate honestly with ourselves and others;

- the styles of communication;

- how to identify irritating listening habits.

We all know that stress is contagious. If we are stressed out at work, we come home wound up and have a less-than-positive attitude towards friends, our husband/wife, children, roommates, etc.

We can minimize the stress contagion and possibly eliminate the stressor if we develop good communication skills in two areas:

1.   with ourselves;

2.   with others.

Communicating with ourselves

Often in stressful situations, what we tell ourselves makes matters worse. The following are the most common pitfalls which occur during conversations with ourselves.

- *Lack of objectivity.*   We believe what we want to believe rather than base our observations on objective information.

- *Responding to 'old tapes'.*   They may not be useful for resolving the current situation or may not contribute to healthy behaviour, but they have helped us cope in the past, so we rely on them when we are under stress.
  For example, when we experience stress and anxiety at work, we tend to withdraw from family and friends. We shut others out, sometimes rudely or brusquely. It may not be healthy behaviour or the best way to deal with the situation, but it accomplishes our objective: People leave us alone.

- *A tendency to blame others.*   If we chronically blame others for our misfortunes or unhappiness, we fail to communicate honestly with ourselves. To some extent, care of the soul asks us to open our hearts wider than they have ever been before, softening the judging and moralism that may have characterized our attitudes and behaviour for years.

● *Convincing ourselves we are victims*. If we decide we are the victims in a stressful situation, we give up any responsibility for controlling or changing it. First, we must accept responsibility for changing the situation; then we can figure out how to make that happen.

● *Focusing on unfairness*. Life isn't fair. Don't spend time beating your chest and feeling put-upon. Accept it.

Understand that the stress produced by calculated or random unfairness is part of life. Evaluate it objectively, take whatever action you can to manage or change the situation, then accept it and move on.

Three ways to communicate honestly with ourselves

1. *Believe we can win*. We must believe we have the power to change or successfully adapt to the situation and must communicate this belief to ourselves, because if we don't believe it, certainly no one else will either.

   One way to develop this perspective, even in our darkest hours, is to look back on situations we believed were very stressful or hopeless one or two years ago. We survived them, didn't we? This is hard evidence that stress and adversity can be overcome – that we can win.

2. *Acknowledge responsibility.* We should be able clearly to identify and admit a problem, then either correct it or, if it's water under the bridge, learn from the experience.

3. *Practice objective evaluation.* We need to identify our biases, prejudices and other sub-jective feelings which may contribute to a stressful situation. If we can separate these feelings and thoughts from the facts, then we can properly evaluate what is really going on.

    For example, you have a personality con-flict with a colleague. You feel mounting stress at the prospect of working with this person. Your pre-existing biases might include the assumption that they will con-tinue to be uncooperative and viewing the relationship as adversarial.

    The facts may be that the past behaviour you identified is accurate, but your colleague has as much interest in getting the project completed as you do; they may feel bad about their past behaviour, etc.

    To practice objective evaluation:

    ●   wipe the slate clean;

    ●   don't assume you'll encounter the same behaviour;

- identify mutual needs;
- determine what you need this person to do to complete the project successfully;
- determine how you will approach the situation to get desired results.

Negative self-talk

Try to avoid negative self-talk – it perpetuates negative stress. Remember, research shows that eight out of ten things we say to ourselves are negative. Work to break the cycle!

Answer 'yes', 'sometimes' or 'no' to the following questions.

1. Do you feel something bad may happen to you?

2. Do you feel you have no power to control what is happening?

3. Do you feel afraid?

4. Do you try to avoid situations or confrontations?

5. Do you take action when something happens?

6. Do you believe you should always do everything right?

7. Do you ask for help when you have difficulty dealing with a problem?

8. Do you have unrealistic expectations of yourself?

9. Do you have trouble saying 'no'?

10. Do you feel everyone should like you?

A large number of 'yes' responses indicates you need to work on communicating honestly with yourself.

Communicating effectively with others

A tremendous amount of interpersonal stress between colleagues and family members could be resolved if even one party practised good communication skills.

The following are three common communication pitfalls that create or perpetuate stress.

1. *Taking it out on others.*   If we lash out at colleagues or our family, become sullen or withdrawn when under stress, we only make a bad situation worse. By not communicating our feelings we leave it to others' imaginations to work out what's wrong. Generally, their conclusions are inaccurate.

2. *Focusing on the symptoms, not the problem.* Too often, when we are under stress, we point to the straw that broke the camel's back as the cause rather than what led to the situation. First, symptoms are easier to identify. Second, they cause the most immediate

temporary relief. At worst, dealing with symptoms heightens the stressful situation and makes communicating with others more difficult.

3. *Reluctance to seek support.* In order to get others' support, we first have to identify what we need from them (understanding, counselling, help for a specific task, etc.). Once we know what we need, we must then explain the problem and how they can help. Most people respond to a well-communicated appeal for help or understanding. They don't respond to erratic or withdrawn behaviour.

Three ways to communicate effectively with others

1. *Tell how you feel.* Communicate clearly and objectively what stress we are experiencing (deadlines, illness, divorce, etc.) when our stressful behaviour affects others or our obligations to them.

   If we're worried about completing a project at work, battling office politics or whatever, tell a wife/husband/friend that we are under a lot of stress and ask for understanding.

2. *Try to identify the real issue.* We all have different perceptions of reality. Checking perceptual filters will help uncloud subjective

views. In a marriage, a spouse's behaviour may be stressful (not hanging up clothes or not washing dishes, etc.), but if these habits haven't been a problem in the past, it is unlikely they are the real issue now. Look deeper. The real issue may be lack of trust or support, a distancing in the relationship or another issue that has slowly developed.

Identify this issue. Then talk it over constructively with the others.

- Point to symptoms objectively as indicators of a more fundamental problem.

- Avoid making accusations.

- Ask for their opinions, observations and ideas for resolving the situation.

- Focus on solutions, not problems.

- Remember the objective is to eliminate stress and restore harmony.

3. *Avoid engaging in conflict.*   People undergoing stress are often unreasonable. Don't respond on an emotional level. Focus on discussing solutions as objectively as possible.

Effective communication techniques to use include the following.

- Let the other party vent their stress.

- Listen closely to pinpoint the underlying issues.

- Try to keep stress in check.

- Give feedback when the other party finishes venting frustration.

- Try to restate the important, fundamental issues in simple, objective, neutral terms.

- Keep the conversation aimed at solutions.

Styles of communication

There are several styles of conflict and communication we use on a daily basis. Consider Table 3.1. Notice how the different behaviours and styles can often lead to conflict.

Take a few minutes to reflect on a conflict you've recently experienced. How did you handle it and what were the results? (It may be helpful to refer to Table 3.1).

1. Describe the conflict or communication. (Who was it with? What was it about?)

2. How did you manage it? (What did you say? How did you act?)

3. What were the results? (How did you feel? How did others feel? Are you happy with the results?)

Now answer the following questions.

Table 3.1   Styles of conflict and communication

	Non-assertive	Directly aggressive	Indirectly aggressive	Assertive
Decision making	Lets others choose	Chooses for others and they know it	Chooses for others, but they don't know it	Chooses for self
Self-sufficiency	Low	High or low	Looks high but usually low	Usually high
Behaviour in problem situations	Flees, gives in	Outright attack	Concealed attack	Direct confrontation
Response of others	Disrespect, guilt, anger, frustration	Hurt, defensiveness, humiliation	Confusion, frustration, feelings of manipulation	Mutual respect
Success pattern	Succeeds by luck or charity of others	Beats others	Wins by manipulation	Attempts 'win–win' solutions

1.   Are you happy with the way you handled your encounter?

2.   Has the conflict/encounter left your relationship stronger or weaker?

3.   What pattern do you recognize in your communication style?

4.   How could you change the way you communicate or deal with conflict?

Irritating listening habits

Identify individuals with whom you are having trouble communicating. Which of the following behaviours affect your ability to communicate with them?

1. They interrupt me when I talk.

2. They ask questions that demand agreement with them; e.g., they make a statement and then say, 'Don't you agree?'.

3. They're always rushed for time, claim to have another meeting to attend and frequently look at their watches while I'm speaking.

4. They give me the feeling that I'm wasting their time.

5. They act as if they are just waiting for me to finish talking so they can interject something of their own.

6. They put me on the defensive when I ask a question or make a suggestion about improving things.

7. They ask questions as if they doubt everything I say.

8. They rarely give me feedback, so I never know if they were listening or if they understood me.

9.   They re-phrase what I say as if I hadn't said it right.

10. They get me off the subject with their questions and comments.

Now, review the list again and make a list of the top three behaviours you want to improve.

Summary

- Stress is often caused, unresolved or worsened by an inability to communicate effectively with ourselves and with others.

- We communicate poorly with ourselves when we:

  1. lack objectivity;

  2. respond to 'old tapes' that may produce unhealthy behaviour;

  3. blame others for causing the stress;

  4. believe we are helpless victims;

  5. focus on life's unfairness.

- We can communicate honestly and productively with ourselves if we:

  1. objectively evaluate the situation and understand how subjective feelings contribute to stress;

2. acknowledge how we contributed to the stressful situation and change our behaviour;

3. believe that we can win; this helps maintain our self-confidence and avoids prolonged anxiety and depression.

● We can't effectively manage a stressful situation unless we can communicate well.

● Common communication pitfalls include:

1. taking stress out on others;

2. focusing on the symptoms, not the problem;

3. a reluctance to ask for support.

● The following are some elements of effective communication.

1. Tell people how we feel. If our stressful behaviour affects others at work or at home, tell them what causes the stress.

2. Try to identify the real issue. When we have identified the issue, talk it over with the others involved. Communicate in a constructive, non-confrontational fashion.

3. Discuss symptoms as indicators of a more fundamental problem.

4. Avoid making accusations.

5. Get their feedback.

6. Communicate that the objective is to achieve harmony.

● If we experience a conflict with another person which produces stress, we should avoid getting involved in a direct confrontation.

1. Let the other party vent his anger.

2. Listen and try to pinpoint the underlying issues.

3. Keep our own stress in check.

4. Give feedback.

5. Restate the fundamental issues.

6. Encourage a dialogue.

7. Keep the conversation aimed at solutions.

4

Stress management techniques

After reading this chapter, you will know:

- five ways to combat job stress;

- relaxation methods to minimize stress;

- how to balance career and family to avoid stress.

Stress-related illnesses and decreased productivity cost British businesses many millions of pounds.

There are five ways to combat job stress. Let's discuss each one in detail.

Five ways to combat job stress

1. *Don't react, act.* Identify the underlying issue. Try to stay objective, especially if other people are involved. Use friends, trusted colleagues and others who may have a valuable perspective to help analyse the situation and identify the basic issues.

2. *Take control.* Again, use carefully selected friends and colleagues to help define and reinforce the course of action. The key is to *do something*.

3. *Learn effective communication skills.* Effective communication means being able to:

    - organize thoughts and key points;

    - express ideas clearly and logically;

    - objectively identify the fundamental stress issues;

    - identify a solution or course of action;

    - identify the benefits of your superior and the company.

4. *Create a means to combat boredom.* Learn why your job is necessary, how it contributes to the company's overall growth and quality of the product, etc.

5. *Know what you like about your job.* Work out how to involve yourself in those aspects,

either by volunteering for additional responsibilities, seeking additional training or
transferring to another department. If you
don't like anything about the job, consider
changing jobs.

Listed below are nine job-related causes of stress.
Make a note of possible solutions to these problems
or issues:

1. unscheduled interruptions;

2. not knowing what to do;

3. no direction;

4. no recognition for work;

5. boredom;

6. no support from team;

7. lack of control;

8. uncertainty about job;

9. can't meet deadlines.

Now make a list of indicators that tell you you're
doing your job well. Then clarify your perception of
'doing your job well' indicators with your manager.
This will help relieve stress and improve both your
productivity and quality of life.

Now, take a moment to complete the checkup
below to identify which area(s) you can do something about.

1. Do you exercise regularly?

2. Is your overall health excellent, good or poor?

3. Have you had your cholesterol checked this year?

4. Are you an ideal weight, over-weight or under-weight?

5. Do you eat a balanced diet?

6. Do you feel depressed or excessively tired?

7. Do you allow yourself down-time to relax each week?

8. Do you suffer from frequent headaches?

9. Do you do aerobic exercises weekly?

10. Have you had your blood pressure checked in the past six months?

Identify the top two areas you plan to improve on. Which one is the most important to take charge of first?

Keep your top improvement priority in mind as you read this chapter.

Stress-free diet

Stress and diet interact in two ways:

1. When we are under stress, our bodies use up

important vitamins and minerals faster. We feel run down mentally and physically. This makes it hard to remain objective about what is causing stress. In addition, our immune systems are adversely affected, making us more susceptible to illness.

2. When we eat poorly, we make it hard for our bodies to withstand the chemical demands of stress. We also put ourselves at risk for illnesses such as heart disease and high blood pressure.

Foods that combat stress

If we are under intense but short-term stress, citrus fruits or other sources of vitamin C will help balance the negative effects of stress.

For ongoing, pervasive stress, we need to supply our bodies continually with protein (lean meat, fish, chicken, nuts, etc.), calcium (milk, yoghurt, cheese, etc.) and potassium (fruits and vegetables).

If we need to settle our nerves when under stress, reach for carbohydrates (sugars and starches). Sweets and biscuits can take your metabolism on a roller-coaster ride from boundless energy to exhaustion. Better choices are foods such as pasta, yogurt, popcorn, nuts, etc.

Stress-aggravating foods

Deep-fried foods high in fat are hard to digest and can make us feel tired. That's why many people are sleepy after a heavy meal.

Depressants and stimulants such as alcohol and caffeine affect the central nervous system. Too much alcohol dehydrates and depletes the body of important vitamins and minerals. The caffeine in coffee and colas can increase tension and anxiety.

Managing stress through relaxation

Relaxation stimulates the body's parasympathetic nervous system, which controls stress responses: respiration, heart rate and digestion. When we relax these areas, we feel more calm.

There are numerous meditation/relaxation programmes available in virtually every form: books, audiotapes, videotapes, workshops, etc. Some may suit some personalities better than others. Try several to find one that works. Meditation should be used after having used relaxation exercises for several weeks.

Relaxation methods

Relaxation methods should be practiced once or twice daily for five to 15 minutes. A quiet, comfortable place and comfortable clothes are essential.

One relaxation method is systematic breathing, which is done by breathing deeply and slowly. The abdomen should push upwards when each breath is started. Exhaling should provide a feeling of warmth and give a heavy, sinking feeling.

Relaxation is not something to 'try to do' – it is letting go of concerns and conflict. With practice, you will be able to switch off and move into the relaxation mode without too much effort. These exercises will allow you to recognize tension or stress and then release it. Ideally, when you go back to your problem, you will be in a more relaxed state to deal with the conflict.

Another good method is relaxing the muscles. Start with the toes; tighten the muscles in the toes and hold for five seconds. Then try to tighten them even further for a few seconds and then let go. This will give a sense of release and will make each muscle feel relaxed. Continue up the body, ending with the face muscles. If a muscle cramp occurs, move on up to the next area. Finally, breathe deeply for a few minutes. Instead of tensing or contracting the different muscles, you can also just let them go limp.

The basic components of most relaxation programmes include the following.

- *Concentration focusing.* The purpose is to concentrate totally on relaxation. Methods used are music, repeating certain words, a guiding voice, a steady or repeating tone or beat, and others.

- *Deep breathing.* The purpose is to counteract and reduce the flow of adrenaline and cortisol in the body. This should feel natural, not forced.

- *Progressive muscle relaxation.* By tensing, then relaxing certain muscles, we become more aware of the tension in our bodies and can consciously reduce it.

- *Gentle muscle stretching*. Feeling loose and relaxed helps you cope with stress more effectively. Methods such as yoga, taichi and other programmes for muscle stretching help achieve this.

- *Visualization/imagery*. By visualizing a peaceful setting and picturing ourselves in it, we can reduce or eliminate much of the mental tension that comes with stress.

- *Music therapy*. Popular choices of music are natural sounds (wind, water, rain, etc.) and music found in the 'New Age' section of record stores.

Working out stress through exercise

Exercise counters the negative effects of stress by:

- limiting the increase in adrenaline triggered by stress;

- allowing the body to react to the 'fight or flight' alarm more efficiently;

- increasing the amount of beta-endorphins in the system – these morphine-like chemicals produce a sense of wellbeing, reduce the sensation of physical pain and counter the effects of negative stress hormones;

- improving circulation and respiration and helping relieve and counter stress. Walking, jogging, rowing, skipping and swimming are good exercises for this.

And now for the step test

The heart-rate taken immediately after exercise is an excellent indicator of aerobic capacity and cardio-vascular condition. This three-minute step test is as accurate in measuring aerobic capacity as are sophisticated treadmill tests. It can be done anywhere, costs nothing and is quite safe.

1. Select a step, bench or stool that is about 12 inches high.

2. The stepping is done in a brisk four-step sequence: up right, up left, down right, down left. Practise performing this at a cadence of 24 sequences per minute (two full sequences every five seconds). Rest for a few minutes.

3. For the actual test, perform the stepping sequence at the set speed for three minutes. Then sit down, wait five seconds and count your pulse for exactly ten seconds (beyond ten seconds, the pulse rate drops rapidly). Compare your count with Table 4.1.

Get started exercising

Find an aerobic activity that can be done for 30 to 40 minutes at least three times a week. You get an

Table 4.1   Ten-second pulse rate

	Women	Men
Excellent	16 or less	17 or less
Good	17–18	18–20
Average	19–22	21–23
Fair	23–25	24–26
Poor	26 or more	27 or more

aerobic workout if your heartbeat ranges from 132 to 176 beats per minute minus your age.

Don't go overboard. Too much exercise can trigger the production of cortisol in the body, which can cause increased stress and other problems.

It has been reported that a person who exercises regularly scores higher on aptitude tests. Exercise also seems to aid in decreasing depression. Try different kinds of exercise to determine which is best for your lifestyle, age and present physical condition. Start slowly and increase activity slowly and consistently.

Stress and changing traditional roles

If we experience stress because of conflicting perceptions about the roles we and our family members assume, here are seven steps we can take to change those roles and the attitudes about them.

1. *Clarify roles and the problems that exist.*

2. *Identify changes to be made.* Don't expect unreasonable changes or make demands as 'pay-back' for past injustices.

3. *Identify areas of conflict and possible solutions.* If we feel it is unreasonable to have to work full time and have complete responsibility for taking care of the house and the children, then identify the area of conflict as 'conflicting demands of three full-time jobs'.
   Possible solutions;

   ● hiring outside help (housekeeper, babysitter, laundry service, etc.);

   ● sharing of jobs among family members;

   ● reduced expectations (laundry will be done less frequently, etc.).

4. *Find out others' expectations.* Pick a time when you and your partner aren't tired or otherwise under stress. Define the problem. Avoid accusations.

5. *Get both parties' wants and needs out in the open.* Look for ways to identify mutual wants and needs. Discuss what roles each person is comfortable with, individually and as a couple.

6. *Discuss possible solutions.* Be prepared to modify original solutions to include partner's suggestions.

7. *Make a stress reduction contract*. Incorporate the mutually acceptable solutions into a 'stress reduction contract' designed to focus on the long-range goal: harmony and a stress-free environment.

Balancing career and family

Look at the statistics.

● Sixty-five per cent of working women and 72 per cent of working men report problems with child care.

● Fifty per cent of these women and 35 per cent of the men say they don't have time for their spouses.

● Fifty per cent of women and 31 per cent of men say they don't spend enough time with their children.

● Sixty-three per cent of the women and 70 per cent of the men report problems associated with having a dual-income family.

Here are some guidelines to help reduce stress in these areas.

● *Decide what's important*. We have to agree on work and home priorities, both individually and as a family. This will, no doubt, involve making difficult choices, many of which involve money.

- *Set limits.*   We can't do it all and neither can our partner. So set limits and discuss them so that expectations are realistic.

- *Learn when to say 'no'.*   Say 'no' when a request or demand is made that conflicts with priorities or exceeds limits that have been set.

- *Don't give in to guilt.*   If we've defined priorities and limits objectively and are willing to stay flexible and co-operate with our partner, there is no reason to feel guilty.

Managing financial stress

In many relationships money is a source of chronic stress and conflict. Money problems tend to fall into two areas:

1.   families living beyond their means;
2.   unexpected financial crisis.

Recent statistics indicate that 44 per cent of young married women with families feel they suffer from financial problems.

Living beyond your means

There are two reasons people live beyond their means:

1.   the availability of credit;

2. trying to create an image or to meet the expectations of others.

It is easy and painless to spend money by relying on credit rather than cash. Unfortunately, stress sets in at the end of the month, when the bills arrive.

Combat financial stress by:

● checking priorities and expectations – are we trying to create an unrealistic (and unafford- able) lifestyle and, if so, why?;

● establishing a budget – if we can create a balanced budget, it becomes an impartial means for settling future spending disputes (the budget, not individual preferences or impulses, then dictates spending decisions);

● creating a savings programme – having money tucked away is insurance against future financial stress should a job loss, emergency, illness or home repair occur.

Weathering a financial crisis

One of the most common financial crises is the unan- ticipated loss of a job. Other financial crises can include catastrophic medical bills or emergency home-repair expenses. Here are five steps to take to manage a financial crisis and reduce accompanying stress.

1. *Identify liquid assets.* This includes houses,

cars, boats, savings accounts, investments, etc. Know how much cash would be available if these items were sold. Also identify how long the liquidation process would take in each case.

2. *Identify monthly expenses.* This should be the absolute minimum required to pay the mortgage, household bills, food, etc. Determine if these expenses can be met with unemployment benefit, savings or other cash on hand.

3. *Discuss options with creditors.* Most creditors are willing to work with a person if the situation is explained. One option is to pay interest only on loans or other obligations for a specific period of time.

4. *Tap into retirement funds.* Some retirement funds can be cashed in early if one is willing to pay a penalty. Others can be used without a penalty. Check with an employer or a retirement fund representative about the restrictions.

5. *Loans against insurance/retirement funds.* Some life insurance policies allow borrowing against the equity accumulated. The same is true in some cases for retirement funds. In both cases, these funds act as collateral that can be borrowed against.

Stress reduction contract

Drawing up a stress reduction contract like the one shown in Figure 4.1 can help you identify the key change that you need to make in order to break the traditional roles you face daily.

I, _____ (name), this _____ (day) of _____

(month)   of   _____   (year),   do   hereby   contract   with

_____(significant other/spouse/children) to:

_____

_____

_____

_____ (significant other/spouse/child) will support

_____ (name) in making this change by:

_____ (specific action)

_____

This contract will be reviewed in:

        7 days _____ (date)
       14 days _____ (date)
       21 days _____ (date)

_____   _____

      Signature   Signature

Figure 4.1   Stress reduction contract

Making it happen

Supposing you read in the paper that an anonymous individual has received the 'Future Money' award in Geneva, Switzerland, and that the individual was quoted as saying, 'My financial independence has been achieved by ...'

How would you complete the story, including what steps this individual took to achieve financial independence (e.g., controls, investments)?

Summary

- There are three ways to reduce the negative effects of stress on a daily basis:

    1. diet;

    2. relaxation;

    3. exercise.

- A well-balanced diet can help manage stress by:

    1. replacing important vitamins and minerals depleted by stress;

    2. making our systems more resistant to the negative effects of stress.

- Certain foods can effectively reverse or moderate the physiological effects of stress.

1. Vitamin C (citrus fruits) helps combat short-term, intense stress.

2. Protein (lean meats, fish, etc.), calcium (milk products) and potassium (vegetables and fruit) help offset the negative effects of long-term stress.

3. Carbohydrates (sugars and starches) can settle nerves. Stick with complex carbohydrates such as pasta, nuts, yoghurt, etc.

●   Some foods can make stress worse.

1. High-fat foods (fatty meats, fried foods, chips, etc.) are hard to digest and can produce fatigue.

2. Alcohol causes mental depression and dehydration and depletes the body of important vitamins and minerals.

3. Caffeine is a stimulant that can cause increased tension.

●   Learning relaxation/meditation techniques can reduce physical and mental stress. Find a programme that complements life-style requirements.

●   Exercise not only reduces the immediate effects of stress, it also conditions the body to withstand hormonal fluctuations.

●   Three areas where people typically experience stress in their personal lives are:

1. interpersonal relationships with family members;

2. balancing career and family obligations;

3. coping with financial problems.

● We can experience stress when we have radically different perceptions from others of the roles and responsibilities each person in the relationship has.

● Managing interpersonal stress requires:

1. good communication;

2. flexibility;

3. co-operation.

● To redefine roles or responsibilities, we need to:

1. clarify roles and existing problems;

2. identify changes we want to make;

3. identify areas of conflict and possible solutions;

4. find out others' expectations;

5. make a stress reduction contract.

● If we experience stress from trying to balance career and family obligations, the following guidelines will help.

1.   establish personal and family priorities;

2.   set limits;

3.   learn to say no to demands on time;

4.   don't give in to guilt.

- Financial problems can cause considerable stress. They are usually the result of:

1.   living beyond our means;

2.   unexpected financial crises.

- If we experience stress because we live beyond our means, we can change by:

1.   establishing a budget;

2.   letting the budget dictate spending decisions;

3.   creating a savings programme.

- Gain control of a financial crisis and reduce the accompanying stress by:

1.   identifying assets;

2.   identifying monthly expenses;

3.   suggesting alternative payment schedules to creditors.

5

Ten commandments for managing stress

There are many steps we can take to combat stress and its unpleasant side effects. The following are ten attitude basics that help fight stress.

1. *Don't let minor aggravations get to us.* We've heard this advice over and over, but it is difficult to practice. There are two things to keep in mind:

    ● *Don't try to ignore feelings of aggravation.* Acknowledge them, then look beyond them to specific solutions or, if that's not possible, review them the next hour, day or week, when the situation may have changed.

- *Keep a sense of perspective.* Small stressors loom large in the present but quickly fade if we let them. Once we understand this, we can see them for what they are: small irritants, not earth-shaking crises.

2. *Don't succumb to guilt.* If we have done something we regret, put it right if possible (apologize, change behaviour, etc.) or learn whatever lessons are available. Don't let others use guilt to manipulate you. If there is a legitimate problem (failed to meet an obligation, hurt someone's feelings, etc.), take steps to make sure it doesn't happen again.

3. *Develop strategies.* Develop an action strategy to achieve a specific solution or a coping strategy for adapting to the situation. In either case, we are not helpless.

4. *Learn to accept and adapt to change.* We can more easily accept and adapt to change if we do the following.

- *Look for the opportunity.* We often focus on solutions which return us to the comfort of the status quo and ignore opportunities that require more energy, effort and flexibility (e.g., moving to take a new job or changing professions).

● *Take a leadership approach.* Don't freeze. Use an action or coping strategy to keep moving. If we've lost a job, we must keep moving. Take an active approach to contacting prospective employers, friends and business colleagues who might act as referrals.

5. *Change the way we look at stress.* Stress is not an external force. Look at stress producers from more than one angle. Look for choices and alternatives. For instance, if we are overwhelmed by an unfamiliar task, we can begin with our existing skills or knowledge. Break the task down into logical steps and work out if and where help is needed. Change focus. View problem solving as enjoyable and challenging.

6. *Develop a support system.* Everyone needs at least one person who acts as a sounding board ... a close friend, family member or professional counsellor. Just verbalizing these feelings eliminates stress. In addition, these people can provide valuable insight and perspective.

7. *Learn to accept the things that can't be changed.* Contemporary society has been spoiled by its ability to control daily life. There are so many things that we can moderate or control that we have little experience, and even less patience, in dealing with those we can't. Our grandparents didn't have this ability to manipulate their environment. They had to

learn to accept things they couldn't change –
untimely death, the weather, crop failures –
and cultivate patience to sustain themselves
until their lives improved.

Learning to accept without losing hope is
a complicated task. How do we do it?

- *See life as cyclical.* Look to the future, when things will improve.

- *Accept our feelings.* If we feel depressed, overwhelmed, anxious or confused, we shouldn't hide those feelings. Use a support system.

- *Keep busy.* Avoid too much free time to think about problems.

- *Change the environment.* Depending on the circumstances, this can be as simple as taking a walk. If the time and money are available, take a trip.

- *Pamper ourselves.* Indulge in a personal luxury (a relaxing hot bath or a small gift).

8. *Develop a personal anti-stress regimen.* The best way to do this involves a combination of diet, exercise and relaxation. An effective programme is:

   - convenient – it should fit easily into our daily schedule;

- time effective – be realistic in the time we can commit;

- inexpensive – activities such as walking are free; a regular programme significantly reduces stress – and expense isn't an excuse.

- enjoyable – don't take up meditation, running or other activities that we have to force ourselves to do; choose activities that are fun.

9. *Don't take it personally.* Others' negative behaviour might be directed towards us, but in many cases we are just convenient targets for the stress, frustration or helplessness they feel. By not taking others' negative behaviour personally, we can break a stress cycle. We shouldn't accept unpleasantness passively. We must assert our right to be treated with respect or temporarily remove ourselves from the situation.

10. *Believe in ourselves.* First and foremost, we must rely on ourselves. In a nutshell, this means believing that, one way or another, we have the inner stamina and fortitude to handle whatever life doles out to us. We must have enough self-confidence to believe we will find the necessary means to withstand stress and look forward to brighter days.

What to do when stress strikes

Next time you are in a stressful situation, ask yourself the following questions.

1. Do I really have a problem?
2. Can I solve the problem?
3. Do I need help with the problem?
4. Do I feel to blame for the problem?
5. Can I change the situation?
6. Am I afraid I can't deal with the problem?
7. Is there really a solution to the problem?
8. Am I in control of the situation?
9. Do I feel the situation is my fault?
10. Am I taking action?

Then make a list of the next three steps you need to take, when to take them and the resource(s) needed.

Index